T0154155

WRITTEN BY GLORIA FOWLER + ILLUSTRATED BY MIN HEO

AMMO

NEW YORK IS ONE OF MY
FAVORITE CITIES OF ALL;

PLEASE COME VISIT,
WINTER, SPRING, SUMMER, OR FALL.

WE CAN SEE THE WHOLE ISLAND
OF MANHATTAN TOGETHER.

COME WITH ME; WE'LL HAVE FUN,
WHATEVER THE WEATHER!

IN THE WINTER:

LET'S GO ICE SKATING
AT ROCKEFELLER CENTER;

LET'S SEE
THE TALL CHRISTMAS TREE
RIGHT WHEN WE ENTER.

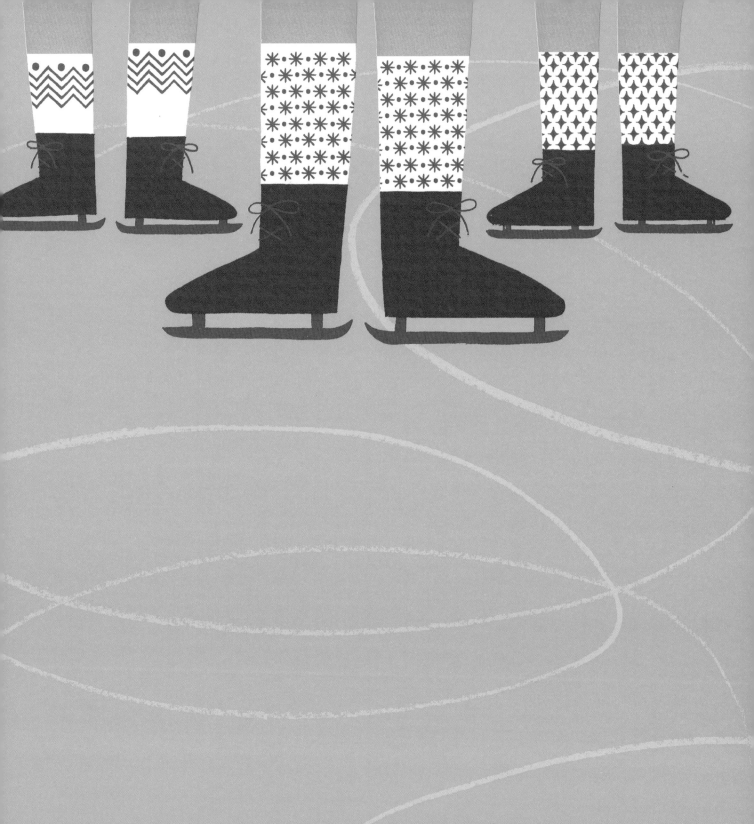

IN THE SPRING:

LET'S ROW A BOAT
ACROSS CENTRAL PARK LAKE;

I'LL BRING SOME SNACKS
AND YOUR FAVORITE CUPCAKES.

IN THE SUMMER:

LET'S SPEND THE DAY
IN CENTRAL PARK.

WE CAN RIDE BIKES,
AND THEN CHASE FIREFLIES
WHEN IT GETS DARK.

IN THE FALL:

LET'S TAKE A BOAT
TO THE STATUE OF LIBERTY;

WE'LL WALK UP TO HER CROWN
AND SEE THE WHOLE CITY.

ALL YEAR LONG:

WE'LL HAVE FUN;
THERE IS SO MUCH TO DO.

SO MANY SIGHTS TO SEE,
MUCH MORE THAN A FEW.

FIRST, LET'S RIDE A TAXI FROM
UPTOWN TO DOWNTOWN—

TAXIS AND TAXIS,
ALL OVER, ACROSS TOWN.

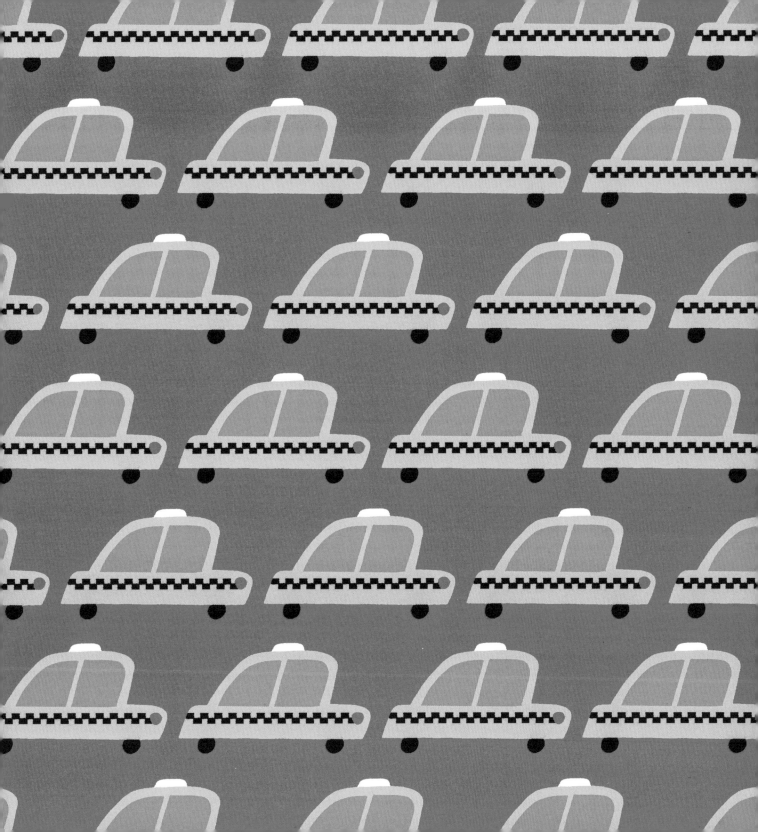

NEXT, LET'S VISIT THE DINOSAURS
AT THE NATURAL HISTORY MUSEUM.

DO THEY WAKE UP AT NIGHT?
I WISH WE COULD SEE THEM.

THEN LET'S VISIT THE TALL BUILDING
CALLED THE EMPIRE STATE.

YOU CAN SEE THE WHOLE CITY.
HURRY UP; I CAN'T WAIT.

HEY, GETTING HUNGRY?
LET'S HAVE SOME PIZZA!

I LOVE NEW YORK;
SO GLAD TO MEETCHA.

LET'S WALK THE BROOKLYN BRIDGE,
ACROSS THE EAST RIVER.

IF IT'S CHILLY, BRING A SWEATER,
OR ELSE YOU MAY SHIVER.

LET'S RIDE THE SUBWAY,
AND TRY NOT TO GET LOST.

THE TRAINS GO SO FAST.
HOLD ON; DON'T GET TOSSED!

AVE

BROADWAY

S SQ

LOOK, HE'S A FIREFIGHTER;
I THINK HE'S THE CAPTAIN.

AND THERE IS A FIRE ESCAPE,
JUST IN CASE SOMETHING HAPPENS.

LET'S SAIL LITTLE BOATS
IN CENTRAL PARK.

WHICH ONE DO YOU WANT?
SO FUN, SUCH A LARK.

LET'S VISIT THE ANIMALS
AT CENTRAL PARK ZOO.

I LOVE THE PENGUINS;
HOW ABOUT YOU?

LET'S RIDE A CAROUSEL,
AROUND AND AROUND.

CENTRAL PARK IS THE BIGGEST
AND BEST PARK IN THIS TOWN.

LET'S TAKE A WALK
ON THE HIGH LINE TOGETHER.

WE CAN STOP FOR GELATO
WHEN THERE'S NICE WEATHER.

LET'S CATCH A TRAIN
AT GRAND CENTRAL STATION:

MORE PEOPLE AND TRAINS
THAN ANYWHERE IN THE NATION.

THERE ARE SO MANY PEOPLE
IN NEW YORK EVERYWHERE.

THEY COME FROM ALL OVER,
FROM HERE AND FROM THERE.

LET'S VISIT THE GUGGENHEIM
AND SEE THE ARTWORK ON VIEW.

WE CAN WALK UP THE SPIRAL,
ALL THE WAY THROUGH.

IS IT TIME FOR A SNACK?
LET'S SEE WHAT WE FIND.

HOT DOGS AND PRETZELS?
I HAD THAT IN MIND.

SEE THE CHRYSLER BUILDING?
THE STYLE IS ART DECO.

THE CURVES AT THE TOP
REPEAT LIKE AN ECHO.

BE CAREFUL CROSSING;
THE STREET IS SO BUSY.

SOOOO MANY CARS;
IT CAN MAKE YOU QUITE DIZZY.

WHAT DO YOU THINK?
IS IT TIME FOR A BREAK?

LET'S TAKE A REST AND
HAVE SOME YUMMY CUPCAKES.

LET'S VISIT TIMES SQUARE
TO SEE ALL THE LIGHTS,

AND THEN SEE A BROADWAY SHOW.
HOW FUN! OUR LAST NIGHT.

I ❤ NY

CAPITAL

THE
EMPIRE
STATE

METROPOLIS
LIFESTYLE

DREAMS

MANHATTAN

TODAY

NYC

MUSICAL

BECOME
A STAR!

AMMO

TWO
thumbs u

NEW YORK

BIG APPLE

MAGICAL

OPENS TONIGHT

SO SAD TO LEAVE,
BUT WE'LL BE BACK SOON.

GOODNIGHT FOR NOW,
AND GOODNIGHT MOON.

FAMOUS SIGHTS FEATURED IN THIS BOOK:

ONE WORLD TRADE CENTER:
THIS SKYSCRAPER WAS BUILT IN 2013. IT IS THE TALLEST BUILDING IN NY AND ONE OF THE TALLEST BUILDINGS IN THE WORLD.

ROCKEFELLER CENTER ICE SKATING RINK:
EVERY WINTER A LARGE CHRISTMAS TREE IS LIT UP NEXT TO THIS FAMOUS ICE SKATING RINK.

CENTRAL PARK:
THIS HUGE URBAN PARK IN THE MIDDLE OF MANHATTAN INCLUDES MANY FUN PLACES FOR KIDS, SUCH AS THE LAKE, CONSERVATORY WATER, CENTRAL PARK ZOO, THE CAROUSEL, AND MANY OTHERS.

THE STATUE OF LIBERTY:
THIS FAMOUS STATUE WAS A GIFT FROM FRANCE IN 1886. SHE HAS GREETED GENERATIONS OF VISITORS AND IMMIGRANTS TO NEW YORK AND AMERICA.

THE SAN REMO:
THE TWO TOWERS OF THIS FAMOUS APARTMENT BUILDING ON THE UPPER WEST SIDE CAN BE SEEN FROM CENTRAL PARK LAKE.

YELLOW CAB TAXIS:
THERE HAVE BEEN TAXIS IN NEW YORK FOR ALMOST A HUNDRED YEARS. TODAY, THERE ARE THOUSANDS OF THEM IN THE CITY.

AMERICAN MUSEUM OF NATURAL HISTORY:
THIS MUSEUM HAS MANY AMAZING DINOSAUR FOSSILS, DIORAMAS, AND OTHER TREASURES.

EMPIRE STATE BUILDING:
THIS FAMOUS SKYSCRAPER WAS BUILT IN 1931 AND STOOD AS THE TALLEST BUILDING IN THE WORLD FOR MANY YEARS.

BROOKLYN BRIDGE:
THIS FAMOUS BRIDGE SPANS THE EAST RIVER AND CONNECTS MANHATTAN TO BROOKLYN. IT IS EASILY RECOGNIZED BY ITS NEO-GOTHIC ARCHES.

NEW YORK CITY SUBWAY:
THIS IS THE LARGEST SUBWAY SYSTEM IN THE WORLD. THE TRAINS RUN 24 HOURS A DAY EVERY DAY OF THE YEAR.

THE HIGH LINE:
THIS FORMER RAILWAY LINE IS NOW AN ELEVATED LINEAR PARKWAY. YOU CAN STILL SEE SOME OF THE RAILROAD TRACKS EMBEDDED IN THE GROUND AND IN THE LANDSCAPE.

GRAND CENTRAL TERMINAL:
THIS BEAUTIFUL BUILDING WAS BUILT IN 1871 AND HAS MORE TRAINS AND PLATFORMS THAN ANY OTHER STATION IN THE WORLD.

THE GUGGENHEIM MUSEUM:
THIS FAMOUS, SPIRAL-SHAPED MUSEUM WAS DESIGNED BY FRANK LLOYD WRIGHT AND BUILT IN 1959.

THE CHRYSLER BUILDING:
THIS WELL-KNOWN HIGH RISE WAS BUILT IN 1930 AND IS RECOGNIZABLE BY ITS JEWEL-LIKE, ART DECO CROWN.

BROADWAY:
THE FAMOUS THEATER DISTRICT IN NEW YORK IS COMMONLY REFERRED TO AS "BROADWAY" FOR THE MAIN STREET THAT RUNS THROUGH THIS AREA.

TIMES SQUARE:
THIS FAMOUS AREA IN MIDTOWN MANHATTAN INCLUDES THE BROADWAY THEATER DISTRICT. THOUSANDS OF TOURISTS COME HERE EVERY YEAR TO SEE PERFORMANCES AS WELL AS ALL OF THE ILLUMINATED BILLBOARDS AT NIGHT.

WRITTEN BY GLORIA FOWLER
ILLUSTRATED BY MIN HEO

ART DIRECTION + DESIGN: GLORIA FOWLER
COPY EDITING: SARA DEGONIA
PRODUCTION: MEGAN SHOEMAKER

SPECIAL THANKS:
STEVE, MILES, AND LOLA CRIST

ISBN: 9781623260507
LOC: 2015904844

FOR MORE CHILDREN'S BOOKS AND PRODUCTS VISIT US AT:
WWW.AMMOBOOKS.COM